William Shake

A Midsummer
Night's Dream

adapted by ALBERT CULLUM

Cover illustration by Phillip Smith

SCHOLASTIC BOOK SERVICES

NEW YORK · TORONTO · LONDON · AUCKLAND · SYDNEY · TOKYO

To the children of Rye, Port Chester, Town of Rye, Harrison, Purchase, who helped celebrate William Shakespeare's 400th birthday.

This edition of "A Midsummer Night's Dream" is reprinted from *Shake Hands with Shakespeare*, a collection of eight plays by Shakespeare adapted by Al Cullum for classroom use in elementary and Junior high schools, and published by Citation Press.

ISBN 0-590-31461-0

10 9 8 7 6 5 4 3 2   1 2 3 4/8
Printed in the U. S. A.   11

Introducing Shakespeare

A *Midsummer Night's Dream* is one of eight plays adapted from Shakespeare by Albert Cullum in the book *Shake Hands with Shakespeare* (Citation Press, 1968). The plays grew out of the author's twenty years of teaching experience in sharing Shakespeare with elementary school classes. In 1964, on the Bard's 400th birthday, Mr. Cullum directed productions of the plays in a special Shakespeare Festival that involved hundreds of students in the public schools in Westchester County, New York.

The author says in his introduction to *Shake Hands with Shakespeare:* "In Elizabethan England certain performances were given at an early hour so young children could attend and return home in time for supper. Why shouldn't today's teachers also expose elementary school children to a touch of the greatness of Shakespeare's poetry and drama?"

The author then gives various suggestions for introducing the play. First, he says, read the script and tell the story (in this case, three interwoven stories) to the class in your own words. Then discuss the story and the characters with the class, reading lines here and there from the play to give the children a taste of Shakespeare's own lyric speech (*My gracious Duke, this man hath bewitched my child*), and to help them in understanding the characters.

When the whole class has become involved is the time for you to read the *script* aloud — and, in the author's words, "feel safe to read in a dramatic style with gestures and bravado." Then, if possible, have the

3

children read the script to themselves and look over the roles to see what parts they'd like to play. Ask for volunteers to read the parts aloud; let them try various roles.

As soon as the children feel comfortable and familiar with the play, you can begin casting. After several classroom rehearsals, when the children are familiar with their lines and roles, let them try a few scenes in the auditorium. *The play's*, after all, *the thing*.

At first there will be fumbling and confusion in the excitement of being on stage, but after a few rehearsals, the actors will be performing as well as they did in the classroom. The scripts — and the production — are flexible. The author tells his actors to ad lib if they forget their lines.

Pointing out that each child in the class will find his place in the production, the author says, "That's the whole purpose of reading and producing Shakespeare — to involve children with great words, great thought, and moods that will inspire them to self-discovery."

THE EDITORS

About the Play

A *Midsummer Night's Dream* has a wonderful combination of fantasy, foolishness, and fun — everyone in the play is a little moonstruck. . . .

There is so much nonsense involved with the everyday characters of the play that laughter will cascade all over the place. The lovers Demetrius, Helena, Lysander, and Hermia are vital to the comic flow of the drama, and, here again, the children will utilize their own sense of horseplay. . . .

A *Midsummer Night's Dream* provides a fine opportunity to develop all types of dances for the fairies of the forest. Let the children begin their creative dancing simply by allowing them to run about, and eventually patterns and movements will develop. The children can compose their own fairy music with mass humming, but if you like, you can always play Mendelsohn's *Midsummer Night's Dream Overture*. When Bottom sings, he can make up a tra-la-la-la song or imitate a rollicking operatic aria.

Of course a feeling of a magical forest is very important to the play. How does one build a forest? The children will have many ideas. One year we had a cloth forest with pieces of cloth cut out in the shapes of trees and pinned against the surrounding drapes. It was a most interesting set, for the various patterns of the cloth gave the forest a definite personality, a strong sense of texture, and a feeling of depth, plus vivid conflicting tones and hues. And it was a forest without one shade of green! Another year the students wanted a feeling of realism, and we scattered and hung about actual tree branches. Children will have many other ideas of how to create the forest if they are given the chance to think and build.

This comic play must move swiftly to keep it frothy, light, and airy.

Costuming and Staging Hints

Costumes for the creatures of the magic forest can be delicate scarves and capes, with strips of chiffon as wands. Any type of light-weight, floating material can readily establish a magical mood. When King Oberon wants to indicate that he is invisible, he can cross his arms in front of his face or partially cover his face with his cloak.

The mortals in the play can wear three-quarter length tunics with a belt around the waist. The royal entourage can wear capes, with the girls in long dresses of any style, but reaching to the ankles.

Now for the very important donkey's head. Please don't go out and rent one — the hired ones are usually so drab and lacking in personality. The school art department may cooperate by helping construct a practical, pretty head, but if there is no cooperative art department, the children can create their own donkey's head in papier mâché.

Except for the opening scene, all the action takes place in the magic forest. I do not close the curtains between scenes but rather empty the stage of actors to indicate a short passage of time.

SCENE 1: In front of the curtain with Egeus "dragging" his daughter down the center or side aisle to present his problem to the ruler, Theseus.

SCENE 2: The curtain opens upon the magic forest.

SCENE 3: This is a good place to present the fairies of the forest in an opening dance. The lighting for the forest when the King and Queen are present should always be mysterious in quality, with lots of dancing shadows.

Scene 4: A bower can be wheeled in for Queen Titania, or two "trees" can be placed together, or two little fairies can hold long branches to represent a bower.

Scene 5: Be sure to have Queen Titania make much love to the donkey's face — the audience will love it. The Queen and Bottom should move up as close to the audience as possible as Titania whispers sweet nothings into the big, long ears.

Scene 6: There is much running about the stage as the two sets of lovers pursue and flee from each other and a great deal of holding, pulling, and pushing.

Scene 7: Still in the magic forest, and again much kissing and exaggerated love-making by Queen Titania.

Scene 8: The staging of the play within a play may appear complicated but is really quite simple. The royal persons and lovers sit comfortably at the back of the stage to watch the performance of the amateur actors. The rustics presenting the play introduce themselves to the real audience and present their play to it. The play itself should be kept extremely simple. For the finale, close the curtains as Puck steps forward to speak the epilogue. If you would like to add an extra treat, after the epilogue open the curtain slowly on a very dimly lit stage where the fairies of the forest are dancing. This is an ideal time and place to use very young children. After a few moments close the curtains again.

A.C.

Characters

THESEUS, Duke of Athens
HIPPOLYTA, betrothed to Theseus
EGEUS, father to Hermia
LYSANDER
DEMETRIUS } in love with Hermia
HERMIA, in love with Lysander
HELENA, in love with Demetrius
PHILOSTRATE, Master of the Revels
PETER QUINCE, a carpenter
SNUG, a joiner
NICK BOTTOM, a weaver
FRANCIS FLUTE, a bellows mender
TOM SNOUT, a tinker
ROBIN STARVELING, a tailor
OBERON, King of the Fairies
TITANIA, Queen of the Fairies
PUCK, a sprite
PEASEBLOSSOM
COBWEB
MOTH } young fairies
MUSTARDSEED
Other fairies attending the King and Queen

A MIDSUMMER NIGHT'S DREAM

Scene 1: The Palace of Theseus in Athens

Theseus, Hippolyta, and Philostrate
are on stage.

THESEUS: Now, fair Hippolyta, our wedding day draws near. Four happy days bring a new moon, but O how slow this old moon wanes.

HIPPOLYTA: Four days will quickly pass, four nights will quickly dream away the time. And then the moon, like a silver bow, shall behold our wedding ceremonies.

THESEUS: Go, Master of Revels. Stir up the Athenian youth to merriments, awake the pert and nimble spirit of mirth, and all Athens shall celebrate. Hippolyta, I wooed thee with my sword, but I will wed thee in another key, with pomp, with triumph, and with revelling.

Enter Egeus and Hermia followed by
Lysander and Demetrius. Exit Philostrate.

EGEUS: Happy be Theseus, our renowned Duke.

THESEUS: Thanks, good Egeus. What's the news?

EGEUS: Full of vexation come I with complaint against my daughter Hermia. Stand forth, Demetrius. My noble lord, this man hath my consent to marry her. Stand forth, Lysander! And my gracious Duke, this man hath bewitched my child. Lysander, thou hast given her love tokens, thou hast by moonlight at her window sung and given her bracelets, rings, nosegays, and sweetmeats. With cunning hast thou stolen my daughter's heart and turned her obedience to stubbornness. And now, my gracious Duke, she will not consent to marry Demetrius. I beg the ancient privilege of Athens — as she is mine, I may dispose of her, which shall be either to this gentleman or to her death, according to our law.

THESEUS: What say you, Hermia? Demetrius is a worthy gentleman.

HERMIA: So is Lysander!

THESEUS: He is, but lacking your father's consent, the other must be held the worthier.

HERMIA: I would my father looked but with my eyes.

THESEUS: Your eyes must look with his judgement.

HERMIA: I do entreat your Grace to pardon me. I am made bold, but may I know the worst that can happen to me if I refuse to wed Demetrius?

THESEUS: Either to die the death, or to abjure forever the society of men. Therefore, fair Hermia, question your desires. Can you endure the life of a nun?

HERMIA: Yes, I will, my Lord, before I ever marry a man I do not love.

THESEUS: Be not hasty, take time to think, and by the new moon either prepare to die for disobedience to your father's will or else to wed Demetrius, or to join a nunnery.

DEMETRIUS: Relent, sweet Hermia, and, Lysander, yield to my certain right!

LYSANDER: You have her father's love, Demetrius. Let me have Hermia's. You marry him!

EGEUS: Scornful Lysander! True, he hath my love, and what is mine, I my love shall grant him. She is mine, and I give her to Demetrius.

LYSANDER: I am, my lord, rich as he, my love is more than his, and Hermia loves me! Why should not I then prosecute my right? Demetrius, I'll say to thy face, made love to Helena and won her soul. The sweet lady is madly in love with him.

THESEUS: I must confess I have heard about that and meant to speak to Demetrius about it. But, Demetrius, come, and come, Egeus, you shall go with me. I have some private matters for you both. For you, fair Hermia, try to see things your father's way. I cannot change the law of Athens. Come, my Hippolyta.

Exit all but Lysander and Hermia.

LYSANDER: How now, my love? Why is your cheek so pale? The course of true love never did run smooth. Listen, Hermia, I have a rich widow aunt and she hath no child. Her house is seven miles away from Athens, and she regards me as her only son. There, gentle Hermia, will I marry thee, and to that place the sharp Athenian law cannot pursue us. Steal out of thy father's house tomorrow night, and in the wood outside the town I'll wait for thee.

Enter Helena.

Look, here comes Helena.

HERMIA: God speed, fair Helena.

HELENA: You call me fair? Demetrius loves you, not me.

HERMIA: The more I hate him, the more he follows me.

HELENA: The more I love him, the more he hates me.

HERMIA: Helena, that is no fault of mine.

HELENA: None but your beauty; would that fault were mine!

HERMIA: Take comfort. He no more shall see my face. Lysander and I will fly away from this place.

LYSANDER: Helena, we'll tell you our secret. Tomorrow night we have decided to elope.

HERMIA: And in the wood where you and I often played, there my Lysander and myself shall meet, and from Athens turn away our eyes to seek new friends and stranger companies. Farewell, sweet playfellow, pray for us, and good luck grant thee thy Demetrius. Good-bye, Lysander, we must not see each other till morrow at midnight.

LYSANDER: All right, my Hermia. (*Exit Hermia.*) Adieu, Helena. I hope Demetrius will learn to love you. (*Exits.*)

HELENA: O, how happy they are! Throughout Athens I am thought as fair as she. But what of that? Demetrius thinks not so. I will tell him of fair Hermia's flight. Then to the wood will he tomorrow night pursue her, and for this intelligence at least, he'll thank me.

Scene 2: The Magic Forest That Night

The six Athenian workmen are gathered together.

QUINCE: Is all our company here?

BOTTOM: You'd better call the role.

QUINCE: Here is the scroll of every man's name, which is thought fit to act in our play before the Duke and Duchess on their wedding night.

BOTTOM: First, good Peter Quince, say what the play is about, then read the names of the actors, and so grow to a point.

QUINCE: All right. Our play is "The Most Lamentable Comedy and Most Cruel Death of Pyramus and Thisby."

BOTTOM: A very good piece of work, I assure you. Now, good Peter Quince, call forth your actors by the scroll.

QUINCE: Answer as I call you. Nick Bottom, the weaver.

BOTTOM: Ready. Name what part I am to play, and proceed.

QUINCE: You, Nick Bottom, are set down for Pyramus.

BOTTOM: Who is Pyramus? A lover or a tyrant?

QUINCE: A lover that kills himself for love.

BOTTOM: I am better in the role of a tyrant. I could play Hercules very well, but I'll also be good as a lover.

QUINCE: Francis Flute, the bellows mender.

FLUTE: Here, Peter Quince.

QUINCE: Flute, you must take Thisby as your role.

FLUTE: What is Thisby? A wandering knight?

QUINCE: It is the lady that Pyramus must love.

FLUTE: Nay, faith, don't make me play a woman. I have a beard coming.

QUINCE: That doesn't matter. You shall play it in a mask and you may speak as small as you can.

BOTTOM: If I may hide my face, let me play Thisby, too. I'll speak in a monstrous little voice...."Ah, Pyramus my lover dear...thy Thisby dear, and lady dear...

QUINCE: No, no. You must play Pyramus. Flute will play Thisby.

BOTTOM: Well, proceed.

QUINCE: Robin Starveling, the tailor.

STARVELING: Here, Peter Quince.

QUINCE: Robin Starveling, you must play Thisby's mother. Tom Snout, the tinker?

SNOUT: Here, Peter Quince.

QUINCE: You, Pyramus' father...myself, Thisby's father. Snug, the joiner, you the lion's part. And I hope here is a play well cast.

SNUG: Have you the lion's part written? If you have, give it to me, for I am a slow study.

QUINCE: You may do it without lines, for it is nothing but roaring.

BOTTOM: Let me play the lion, too! I will roar that it will do any man's heart good to hear me. I will roar so well that the Duke will say, "Let him roar again, let him roar again."

QUINCE: If you should do it too terribly, you would so fright the Duchess and the ladies that they would shriek, and that were enough to hang us all.

ALL: That would hang us all, every mother's son.

BOTTOM: I grant you, friends, if you should frighten the ladies out of their wits, they would hang us, but I will aggravate my voice so that I will roar you as gently as any kitten.

QUINCE: You can play no part but Pyramus, for Pyramus is a sweet-faced man, a proper man, a most lovely gentlemanlike man. Therefore, you must play Pyramus.

BOTTOM: Well, I will undertake it. What beard were I best to play it in?

QUINCE: Why, whatever you like.

BOTTOM: I will play it in either your straw color beard, your orange-tawny beard, your purple-in-grain beard, or your yellow beard.

QUINCE: Masters, here are your parts, and I request you to memorize them by tomorrow night, and meet me in the palace wood a mile without the town, by moonlight. There will we rehearse, for if we meet in the city, we shall be dogged with company. In the meantime, I will draw a list of properties such as our play needs. I pray you, fail me not.

BOTTOM: We will meet, and there we may rehearse most wonderfully. Take pains, be perfect. Adieu.

QUINCE: At the Duke's oak we meet. (*All exit.*)

Scene 3: The Forest the Following Night

Puck and fairies enter from opposite sides
of stage.

PUCK: How now, spirit, whither wander you?

FIRST FAIRY: Over hill, over dale,
    Through bush, through brier
    Over park, over pale,
    Through flood, through fire.
    I do wander everywhere,
    Swifter than the moon's sphere
    And I serve the Fairy Queen.
    I must go seek some dewdrops here,
    And hang a pearl in every cowslip's ear.
    Farewell, I'll be gone,
    Our Queen and all her elves come here
      soon.

PUCK: The King doth keep his revels here tonight. Take heed the Queen come not within his sight. For Oberon is full of wrath because she had stolen a lovely boy from an Indian king, and jealous Oberon would have the child, but she witholds the loved boy, crowns him with flowers and makes him all her joy. And now they never meet but they do so fuss, that all their elves hide for fear.

FIRST FAIRY: Either I mistake your shape, or else you are that shrewd and knavish sprite called Robin Goodfellow. Are not you he that misleads night wanderers, laughing at their confusion? Those that call you sweet Puck, you do their work and they shall have good luck. Are not you he?

PUCK: That's right. I am that merry wanderer of the night. I jest to Oberon and make him smile . . . and here comes Oberon.

FIRST FAIRY: And here, my mistress.

Enter Oberon and Titania from opposite sides.

OBERON: Ill met by moonlight, proud Titania.

TITANIA: What? Jealous Oberon? Fairies, let us go. I have forsworn his company.

OBERON: Tarry, rash Titania. Am I not thy lord?

TITANIA: Then I must be thy lady. Never since the middle summer's spring met we, but with thy brawls thou hast disturbed our sport. Therefore the spring, the summer, the autumn, angry winter change their appearance, and the amazed world knows not which season is which. This is what comes of our dissension. We are the cause.

OBERON: You amend it then. It is your fault. Why should Titania cross her Oberon? I do but beg a little changeling boy to be my henchman.

TITANIA: Set your heart at rest, the fairyland buys not the child of me. His mother was my friend and, for her sake, do I rear up her boy, and I will not part with him.

OBERON: How long within this wood do you intend to stay?

TITANIA: Perhaps till after Theseus' wedding day. If you will patiently dance in our round and see our moonlight revels, go with us. If not, shun me, and I will spare your haunts.

OBERON: Give me that boy, and I will go with thee.

TITANIA: Not for thy fairy kingdom. Fairies, away! We shall argue more, if I longer stay.

Exit Titania and her fairies.

OBERON: Well, go thy way. Thou shalt be sorry for this. My gentle Puck, come hither. Fetch me *that* flower, the herb I showed thee once. The juice of it on sleeping eyelids laid will make a man or woman fall madly in love with the next live creature that it sees. Fetch me this herb, and be thou here again quickly.

PUCK: I'll put a girdle about the earth in forty minutes. (*Exits.*)

OBERON: Having once this juice, I'll watch Titania when she is asleep and drop the liquor of it in her eyes. The next thing then she, waking, looks upon, be it lion, bear, or meddling monkey, she shall pursue it with the soul of love. And before I take this charm off from her sight, as I can take it with another herb, I'll make her render up her page to me. But who comes here? I am invisible, and I will overhear their conference.

Enter Demetrius followed by Helena.

DEMETRIUS: I love thee not; therefore pursue me not. Where is Lysander, and fair Hermia? You told me they were stolen unto this wood. Stop following me!

HELENA: You draw me like a magnet. Leave your power to draw, and I shall have no power to follow you.

DEMETRIUS: Do I entice you? Or rather do I not in plainest truth tell you I do not, nor I cannot, love you?

HELENA: And even for that, do I love you the more. Demetrius, spurn me, neglect me, only let me follow you.

DEMETRIUS: Tempt not too much the hatred of my spirit, for I am sick when I do look at you.

HELENA: And I am sick when I look not on you.

DEMETRIUS: You must return to the city, a young girl like you should not be out at night alone.

HELENA: It is not night when I do see your face, nor doth this wood lack worlds of company, for you are all the world. Then how can you say I am alone, when all the world is here?

DEMETRIUS: I'll run from thee, and hide, and leave thee to the mercy of the wild beasts.

HELENA: The wildest hath not such a heart as you.

DEMETRIUS: I will not stay. . . . Let me go, and don't follow me! (*Exits.*)

HELENA: Ay, in the town, in the field, I'll follow thee. (*Exits*).

OBERON: Fare thee well, young lady. Before he leaves this grove, thou shalt run from him, and he shall seek thy love.

Enter Puck.

Hast thou the flower there?

PUCK: Ay, there it is.

OBERON: Give it to me. I know a bank where the wild flowers grow. . . . There sleeps Titania, and with juice of this I'll streak her eyes. Take some of it, and seek through this grove . . . A sweet Athenian lady is in love with a disdainful youth. Anoint his eyes, but do it when the next thing he sees may be the lady. You will know the man by the Athenian garments he hath on.

PUCK: Fear not my lord your servant shall do so.

(Both exit.)

Scene 4: The Bower of Titania an Hour Later

Enter Titania and her fairies.

TITANIA: Come, now a fairy song. Sing me now asleep, then let me rest.

FIRST FAIRY: You spotted snakes, with double tongue,
Thorny hedgehogs, be not seen,
Newts and blind worms do no wrong,
Come not near our Fairy Queen.

FAIRY CHORUS: Lulla, lulla, lullaby, lulla, lulla, lullaby.

SECOND CHORUS: Weaving spiders come not here,
Away you long-legged spinners, hence!
Beetles black approach not here,
Worm nor snail do no offence.

FAIRY CHORUS: Lulla, lulla, lullaby, lulla, lulla, lullaby.

THIRD FAIRY: Away, now all is well.

Exit fairies; enter Oberon who tiptoes over to Titania and squeezes the flower juice on her eyelids.

OBERON: What thou seest, when thou dost awake, do it for thy true love take. Love and languish for his sake. Be it cat or bear, leopard, or boar with bristled hair. Wake when some vile thing is near!

Exit Oberon; enter Lysander and Hermia.

LYSANDER: Fair love, you faint with wandering in the wood, and to tell the truth, I have lost our way. We will rest, Hermia, if you think it best.

HERMIA: Be it so, Lysander. Find yourself a bed, for I upon this bank will rest my head.

LYSANDER: One turf shall serve as pillow for us both.

HERMIA: No, Lysander, for my sake, my dear, lie further off yet, do not lie so near.

LYSANDER: All right. Here is my bed. . . . Sleep give thee rest.

HERMIA: Good night!

Enter Puck.

PUCK: Through the forest have I gone, but Athenian found I none on whose eyes I might drop this flower's magic. (*See Lysander.*) Ah! Who is here? Clothes of Athens he doth wear. This is he who, my master said, despised the Athenian maid, and here the maiden sleeping sound. (*He squeezes the flower on Lysander's eyelids.*) Upon the eyelids I throw all the power this charm doth owe. So, awake when I am gone, for I must now to Oberon.

Exit Puck; enter Demetrius and Helena running.

HELENA: Sweet Demetrius, wait!

DEMETRIUS: I charge thee, get away and do not haunt me thus.

HELENA: O wilt thou leave me? Do not so.

DEMETRIUS: Stay on thy peril. I alone will go. (*Exits.*)

HELENA: O, I am out of breath.... But who is here? Lysander, on the ground? Dead, or asleep? I see no blood, no wound. Lysander, if you live, good sir, awake.

LYSANDER (*awaking*): And run through fire I will for thy sweet sake. Where is Demetrius? He shall perish on my sword.

HELENA: Do not say so, Lysander, say not so. Hermia still loves you . . . then be content.

LYSANDER: Content with Hermia? No, not Hermia, but Helena I love. Who will not change a raven for a dove?

HELENA: Why do you mock me? When at your hand did I deserve this scorn? Is it not enough that I never can deserve a sweet look from Demetrius? You do me wrong. Fare you well. I thought you of more true gentleness. (*Exits.*)

LYSANDER: Helena! (*Chases after her.*)

HERMIA (*awakening*): Help me, Lysander, help me! What a dream was here! Lysander, look how I do quake with fear. Lysander! What, out of hearing? Gone? No sound, no word? Alack, where are you? I faint almost with fear. Either death, or you I'll find immediately. (*Exits.*)

Scene 5: Same Spot in the Forest a Little Later

Titania is lying asleep. Enter Quince, Snug,
Bottom, Flute, Snout, and Starveling.

BOTTOM: Are we all here?

QUINCE: Here's a marvelous place for our rehearsal. This green plot shall be our stage, this hawthorn bush our dressing room, and we will do it in action as we will do it before our Duke.

BOTTOM: Peter Quince?

QUINCE: Yes, Bottom.

BOTTOM: There are things in this comedy of Pyramus and Thisby that will never please. First, Pyramus must draw a sword to kill himself, which the ladies cannot abide. How answer you that?

STARVELING: I believe we must leave the killing out when all is done.

BOTTOM: I have a device to make all well. Write me a prologue, and let the prologue seem to say we will do no harm with our swords and that Pyramus is not killed indeed. And for better assurance, tell them that I Pyramus am not Pyramus, but Bottom the weaver . . . this will put them out of fear.

QUINCE: Well, we will have such a prologue.

SNOUT: Will not the Ladies be afraid of the lion?

STARVELING: I'm afraid so.

BOTTOM: Masters, to bring in a lion among ladies is a most dreadful thing for there is not a more fearful wild fowl than your lion living, and we ought to look into it.

SNOUT: Therefore, another prologue must tell he is not a lion.

BOTTOM: Nay, and half his face must be seen through the lion's neck and he himself must speak through saying thus, "Ladies, O fair ladies, you think I come hither as a lion . . . no, I am no such thing, I am Snug, the joiner."

QUINCE: Well, it shall be so. But there are two hard things . . . that is, to bring the moonlight into a chamber, for you know Pyramus and Thisby meet by moonlight.

SNUG: Doth the moon shine the night we play our play?

BOTTOM: A calendar, a calendar! Look in the almanac. Let us see if the moon doth shine.

QUINCE: Yes, it doth shine that night.

BOTTOM: Why then, may you leave a casement of the great chamber window where we play open, and the moon may shine in at the casement.

QUINCE: Ay, or else one must come in with a lantern

and say he comes to represent the person of moon-shine. Then, there is another thing we must have ... we must have a wall in the great chamber, for Pyramus and Thisby, says the story, did talk through the chink of a wall.

SNOUT: You can never bring in a wall. What say you, Bottom?

BOTTOM: Some man or other must represent the wall, and let him hold his fingers thus, and through the cranny shall Pyramus and Thisby whisper.

QUINCE: If that may be, then all is well. Come, sit down everybody and rehearse your parts. Pyramus, you begin, and so everyone according to his cue.

Enter Puck.

PUCK: What have we here, so near the cradle of the Fairy Queen? What? A play in rehearsal? I'll listen, and be an actor, too, perhaps, if I see a cause.

QUINCE: Speak, Pyramus. Thisby, stand up.

BOTTOM: Thisby, the flowers of odious savours sweet ...

QUINCE: Odours, odours!

BOTTOM: — Odours savours sweet. So hath thy breath, my dearest Thisby sweet. But hark, a voice ... stay thou but here awhile, and by and by I will to thee appear. (*Exits.*)

PUCK: (*aside*): A stranger Pyramus than e'er played here! (*Exits.*)

FLUTE: Must I speak now?

QUINCE: Ay, you must. For you must understand he goes but to see a noise that he heard, and is to come again.

FLUTE: Most radiant Pyramus, most lily-white of hue,

as true as truest horse that yet would never tire, I'll meet thee, Pyramus, at Ninny's tomb.

QUINCE: Ninus' tomb, man! Why you must not speak that yet — that you answer to Pyramus. You speak all your parts at once, cues and all. Pyramus enter, your cue is past; it is "never tire."

FLUTE: O, that yet would never tire.

Enter Puck and Bottom wearing an Ass's head.

BOTTOM: If I were fair, Thisby, I were only thine!

QUINCE: O monstrous! O strange! We are haunted. Pray masters, fly! HELP!

Exit Quince, Snug, Flute, Snout, and Starveling.

PUCK: I'll follow you. I'll lead you about around, through bog, through bush, through brier. Sometime a horse I'll be, sometime a hound, and neigh and bark at every turn. (*Exits.*)

BOTTOM: Why do they run away? This is a trick of theirs to make me afraid.

Re-enter Snout and Quince.

SNOUT: O Bottom, thou art changed, What do I see on thee?

BOTTOM: What do you see?

QUINCE: Bless thee, Bottom, bless thee. Thou art transformed!

Snout and Quince run out.

BOTTOM: I see their knavery! This is to make an ass of me, to frighten me if they could. But I will not stir from this place, do what they can. I will walk up and down here, and will sing, that they shall hear that I am not afraid. (*Begins to sing.*)

TITANIA (*awaking*): What angel wakes me from my flower bed?

Bottom sings again.

I pray thee, gentle mortal, sing again. Mine ear is much enamoured of thy note. So is mine eye enthralled to thy shape, and thy beauty doth move me on the first view to swear I love thee.

BOTTOM: Methinks, mistress, you should have little reason for that. And yet, to say the truth, reason and love keep little company together nowadays.

TITANIA: Thou art as wise as thou art beautiful.

BOTTOM: Not so neither, but if I were I'd get out of this wood.

TITANIA: Out of this wood do not desire to go. Thou shalt remain here, whether thou wilt or no. I do love thee, therefore go with me. I'll give thee fairies to attend thee, and they shall sing while thou on pressed flowers do sleep: Peaseblossom, Cobweb, Moth, and Mustardseed!

Enter four little fairies.

PEASEBLOSSOM: Ready!

COBWEB: And I!

MOTH: And I!

MUSTARDSEED: And I!

ALL: Where shall we go?

TITANIA: Be courteous to this gentleman. Feed him with apricots and dewberries; the honey bags steal from the bumblebees. Nod to him, elves, and do him courtesies.

PEASEBLOSSOM: Hail, mortal.

ALL: Hail, mortal!

BOTTOM: What's your name?

COBWEB: Cobweb.

BOTTOM: I shall desire more of your acquaintance, good Master Cobweb. Your name, honest gentleman?

PEASEBLOSSOM: Peaseblossom.

BOTTOM: I pray you, commend me to Mistress Squash, your mother, and to Master Stringbean, your father. Your name, I beseech you, sir?

MUSTARDSEED: Mustardseed.

BOTTOM: Good Master Mustardseed, I know you well. You make my eyes water. I desire to know you better, good Master Mustardseed.

TITANIA: Come, wait upon him. Lead him to my bower, tie up my love's tongue . . . bring him silently. (*All exit.*)

Scene 6: Another Part of the Forest a Few Minutes Later

Enter Oberon.

OBERON: I wonder if Titania has awakened?

Enter Puck.

Here comes my messenger. How now, mad spirit?

PUCK: My mistress with a monster is in love. Near to her bower, while she was sleeping, a crew of actors met together to rehearse a play intended for great Theseus' wedding day. The dumbest one of the lot who played Pyramus forsook his scene and entered in the forest where I fixed on his head, the head of a jackass. When the rest saw him, they all ran away. I left sweet Pyramus there when in that moment Titania woke up and immediately fell in love with a jackass.

OBERON: This falls out better than I imagined it would.

But hast thou yet latched the Athenian's eyes with the love juice as I told thee to do?

PUCK: I did while he was sleeping, and the Athenian woman by his side that, when he waked, by force she must be eyed.

Enter Hermia and Demetrius.

OBERON: Stand close, this is the same Athenian.

PUCK: This is the woman, but this is not the man.

DEMETRIUS: O, why rebuke me when I love you so?

HERMIA: If thou hast slain Lysander in his sleep, plunge in the knife and kill me too. It cannot be that thou hast murdered him. Where is my Lysander? Ah, good Demetrius, wilt thou give him to me?

DEMETRIUS: I had rather give his carcass to my hounds.

HERMIA: Hast thou slain him, then? Henceforth be never numbered among men. Hast thou killed him sleeping?

DEMETRIUS: No, I am not guilty of Lysander's blood, nor is he dead that I know of.

HERMIA: I pray thee, tell me where he is!

DEMETRIUS: And if I could, what should I get for it?

HERMIA: A privilege, never to see me more, whether he be dead or no! (*Exits.*)

DEMETRIUS: There is no following her in this fierce vein. Here, therefore, for a while I will remain. So sorrow's heaviness doth heavier grow. O, I am sleepy. (*Lies down and sleeps.*)

OBERON (*to Puck*): What hast thou done? Thou hast made a mistake! And laid the love juice on some true love's sight. This is true love turned, and not a false turned true.

PUCK: I'm sorry, master. Can we mend it?

OBERON: Go swifter than the wind and find Helena of Athens. She is sick with sighs of love. By some illusion bring her here. I'll charm his eyes till she doth appear.

PUCK: I go, I go! Look how I go! Swifter than an arrow from a bow. (*Exits.*)

OBERON (*squeezes the flower on Demetrius*): Flower of this purple dye, sink in the apple of his eyes. When thou wakest, if she be by, thou shalt love her eye to eye.

Re-enter Puck.

PUCK: Helena is here at hand, and the youth, mistook by me, pleading for her love. Shall we watch? Lord, what fools these mortals be!

OBERON: Stand aside. The noise they make will cause Demetrius to wake.

PUCK: Then will both of them love her! (*Much laughter.*)

Enter Helena and Lysander.

LYSANDER: Why should you think that I woo in mockery. Look, when I vow, I weep.

HELENA: You're making fun of me. You love only Hermia.

LYSANDER: No, Demetrius loves her, and he loves not you.

DEMETRIUS (*awaking*): O Helena, goddess divine! To what, my love, shall I compare thee? O, let me kiss you.

HELENA: I see you all are bent on making fun of me for your merriment. How can you treat me this way! You both are rivals and love Hermia, and now both rival to mock Helena.

LYSANDER: You are unkind, Demetrius, for you love

Hermia. This you know I know. And here, with all my heart, in Hermia's love I yield you up my part. I do love Helena and will till death.

HELENA: This is monstrous!

DEMETRIUS: Lysander, keep Hermia. If I loved her, all that love is gone. Now I love Helena.

LYSANDER: Helena, it is not so.

DEMETRIUS: Disparage not my love. Look, here comes thy love. Yonder is thy dear.

Enter Hermia.

HERMIA: Lysander, why did you leave me so unkindly?

LYSANDER: Why should I stay, when love doth call me! I love fair Helena! Why do you seek me?

HERMIA: You speak not as you think. It cannot be.

HELENA: Lo! She is one of this confederacy. Now I perceive they have joined all three to fashion this false sport in spite of me. Injurious Hermia, have you conspired with these men in scorning your poor friend? It is not friendly.

HERMIA: I am amazed. I scorn you not. It seems that you scorn me.

HELENA: Have you not sent Lysander to follow me and to praise my eyes and face? And made your other love, Demetrius, to call me goddess divine?

HERMIA: I understand not. What do you mean by this?

HELENA: That's right, keep up the show, counterfeit sad looks. Make faces at me when I turn my back. Wink at each other . . . laugh at me! If you have any pity or manners, you would not tease me so. But fare ye well, 'tis partly mine own fault!

LYSANDER: Stay, gentle Helena, hear my excuse. My love, my life, my soul, fair Helena.

HELENA: Stop it!

HERMIA: Sweet, do not tease her so.

DEMETRIUS: If she cannot entreat, I can compel.

LYSANDER: Thou canst compel me no more than she entreat. Helena, I love thee, by my life, I do.

DEMETRIUS: I say I love thee more than he can do.

LYSANDER: Then prove it with your sword. Come with me.

DEMETRIUS: Gladly! After you!

HERMIA: Lysander, what does this mean?

LYSANDER: Go ahead, Demetrius!

Hermia throws her arms around Lysander.

DEMETRIUS: You are a coward!

LYSANDER: Coward! *(to Hermia)* Take your hands off me, or I will shake thee from me like a serpent.

HERMIA: Why are you grown so rude? What change is this, sweet love?

LYSANDER: Thy love? Out loathed medicine! O hated potion, away.

HERMIA: Do you not jest?

HELENA: Yes, of course he does, and so do you.

LYSANDER: Demetrius, I will keep my word with you.

DEMETRIUS: I would I had your bond, for I perceive a weak bond holds you. I'll not trust your word.

LYSANDER: Why should I hurt her, strike her, kill her dead? Although I hate her, I'll not harm her so.

HERMIA: What? Can you do me greater harm than hate? Hate me . . . why? Am I not Hermia? Are you not Lysander? I am as fair now as I was before. Why then you left me on purpose?

LYSANDER: Yes! And never did desire to see thee more. Therefore, be certain it is no jest that I do hate thee, and love Helena.

HERMIA (*to Helena*): O, you thief of love! You have come by night and stolen my love's heart from him.

HELENA: Why, why . . . you counterfeit . . . you puppet, you!

HERMIA: Puppet? (*Attempts to attack Helena.*)

HELENA: I pray you, gentlemen, let her not hurt me . . . let her not strike me.

LYSANDER: Be not afraid. She shall not harm thee.

DEMETRIUS: No sir, she shall not.

HELENA: When she's angry, she is keen and shrewd. She was a vixen when she went to school, and though she be but little, she is fierce.

HERMIA: Why will you let her insult me so? Let me at her!

LYSANDER (*to Hermia*): Get you gone, you dwarf, you midget, you bead, you acorn!

DEMETRIUS: Who asked you to speak for Helena? Take not her part.

LYSANDER: Now she holds me not. Now follow, if thy darest. I'll show you who has a right to take up for Helena.

DEMETRIUS: I'll follow thee!

Exit Lysander and Demetrius.

HELENA (*to Hermia*): I will not trust you. . . . I no longer stay in your curst company. Your hands than mine are quicker for a fray. My legs are longer though, to run away! (*Exits.*)

HERMIA: I am amazed, and know not what to say! (*Exits.*)

OBERON: Is this another mistake? Or did you do this on purpose?

PUCK: Believe me, king of shadows, I mistook. Did not

you tell me I should know the man by the Athenian garments he had on?

OBERON: Thou seest these lovers seek a place to fight, therefore lead these rivals so astray as one come not within another's way, and put them to sleep. Then crush this herb into Lysander's eye, whose liquid hath this quality to take from thence all error with his sight. When they awake, all this shall seem a dream, and back to Athens shall the lovers go. I'll to my queen and beg her Indian boy, and then I will her charmed eye release from monster's view, and all things shall be peace.

PUCK: My fairy lord, this must be done with haste, for night's beauty is nearly over. . . . It will soon be dawn.

OBERON: Make no delay. We may effect this business yet before day. (*Exits.*)

PUCK: Here comes one of them.

Re-enter Lysander.

LYSANDER: Where are thou, proud Demetrius? Speak thou now! The villain is much lighter heeled than I. I followed fast, but faster he did fly. O, I am tired. I'll rest a little then in the morning I'll find Demetrius and achieve my revenge. (*Lies down and sleeps.*)

Re-enter Demetrius.

DEMETRIUS: Where art thou, Lysander? If ever thy face I see! Faintness constraineth me to measure out my length on this cold bed. (*Lies down and sleeps.*)

Re-enter Helena.

HELENA: O weary night, o long and tedious night, abate thy hours. Shine comforts from the east, that I may back to Athens by daylight. And sleep, that sometime shuts up sorrow's eye, steal me awhile from mine own company. (*Lies down and sleeps.*)

PUCK: Yet but three? Come, one more. Two of both kinds makes up four. Here she comes, curst and sad. Cupid is a knavish lad, thus to make poor females mad.

Re-enter Hermia.

HERMIA: Never so weary, never so in woe, bedabbled with the dew and torn with briers. I can no further crawl, no further go. My legs can keep no pace with my desires. Here will I rest me till the break of day. Heavens shield Lysander, if they have a fray. (*Lies down and sleeps.*)

PUCK: On the ground sleep sound. I'll apply to your eye, gentle lover, remedy. (*Squeezes the herb on Lysander's eyelids.*) When thou wakest, thou takest true delight in the sight of thy former lady's eye. Jack shall have a Jill, naught shall go ill, and all shall be well.

Scene 7: Titania's Bower in the Forest Early the Next Morning

Enter Titania, Bottom, and the fairies.
Oberon is hiding in the background.

TITANIA: Come sit thee down upon this flowery bed, while I thy amiable cheeks do coy, and stick muskroses in thy smooth head, and kiss thy fair large ears, my gentle joy.

BOTTOM: Where's Peaseblossom?

PEASEBLOSSOM: Ready.

BOTTOM: Scratch my head, Peaseblossom. Where is Master Cobweb?

COBWEB: Ready.

BOTTOM: Where is Master Mustardseed?

MUSTARDSEED: What is your will?

BOTTOM: Nothing, but to help Peaseblossom and Cobweb to scratch. I must to the barber's, for methinks I am marvellous hairy about the face. And I am such a tender jackass, if one hair do but tickle me, I must scratch.

TITANIA: Wilt thou hear some music, my sweet love?

BOTTOM: I have a reasonable good ear in music. Let's have some music.

TITANIA: Or say, sweet love, what thou desirest to eat.

BOTTOM: Truly, a peck of good dry oats. Methinks I have a great desire to a bottle of hay.

TITANIA: I have a venturous fairy that shall seek the squirrel's hoard and fetch thee new nuts.

BOTTOM: I had rather have a handful or two of dried peas. But, I pray you, let none of your people stir me. I have a feeling of sleep come upon me.

TITANIA: Sleep thou, and I will wind thee in my arms. Fairies be gone. (*Exit all the fairies.*) O how I love thee! How I dote on thee! (*They sleep.*)

    Oberon steps forward and Puck enters.

OBERON: Welcome, good Puck. Seest thou this sweet sight? Her dotage now I do begin to pity. For now I have the boy, I will undo this hateful imperfection of her eyes. And, gentle Puck, take this transformed scalp from off the head of this Athenian, that he, awakening when the others do, may all go back to Athens and think of this night's accidents as a merry dream. But first I will release the Fairy Queen. (*Touches her eyes with an herb.*) Now my Titania, wake you, my sweet Queen.

TITANIA: My Oberon, what visions have I seen! Methought I was in love with a jackass!

OBERON: There lies your love!

TITANIA (*screaming*): How came these things to pass? O, how mine eyes do loathe his visage now.

OBERON: Silence awhile. Puck, take off his head. Titania, music call, to wake these five from their charmed sleep. (*Music swells.*) Come, my Queen, take hands with me, and rock the ground whereon these sleepers be. We will tomorrow midnight dance in Duke Theseus' house, and there shall the pairs of faithful lovers be wedded with Theseus.

PUCK: Fairy King, attend and mark.... I do hear the morning lark.

OBERON: Then, my Queen, trip we after night's shade, swifter than the wandering noon.

TITANIA: Come, my lord, and tell me how it came about that I sleeping here was found with these mortals on the ground!

Exit Oberon, Titania, and fairies.
Enter Theseus and Egeus.

EGEUS: There they are, my lord. This is my daughter here asleep, and this is Lysander. Enough, my lord. You have seen enough. I beg the law, the law upon his head! (*The lovers awake.*) They would have stolen away, they would, Demetrius, thereby to have defeated you and me.

DEMETRIUS: But, my lord, I love Helena, and she loves me. My love to Hermia melted as the snow.

THESEUS: Fair lovers, you are fortunately met. Of this discourse we more will hear anon. Egeus, in the temple, by and by, these couples shall be eternally knit. We will hold a feast. Come along everyone.

All exit except Bottom.

BOTTOM: (*awaking*): When my cue comes, call me, and I will answer. Heigh ho! Peter Quince? Flute, the bellows mender? Snout, the tinker? Starveling? They stole away and left me asleep. I have had a most rare dream! Methought I was...a... (*Runs off.*)

Scene 8: Theseus' Palace That Evening

Enter Hippolyta, Theseus, and Philostrate.

HIPPOLYTA: 'Tis strange, my Theseus, the story that these lovers told.

THESEUS: More strange than true. I never believe these fairy stories. It was only their imaginations.

Enter Lysander, Demetrius, Hermia, and Helena.

Here comes the lovers, full of mirth and joy. Gentle friends, come now. What masks, what dances shall we have? Where is our usual manager of mirth? What revels are in hand? Is there no play?

PHILOSTRATE: Here, mighty Theseus, here is a list. Make choice of which Your Highness will see first.

THESEUS: A tedious brief scene of young Pyramus and his love Thisby...very tragical mirth? Merry and tragical? Tedious and brief? What are they that do play it?

PHILOSTRATE: Hard handed men that work in Athens here.

THESEUS: I will hear that play. For never anything can be amiss when simpleness and duty tender it. Go bring them in, and all take your places.

PHILOSTRATE: So please Your Grace, the prologue is ready.

THESEUS: Let him approach.

Trumpets sound. Enter Quince as the Prologue,
Bottom as Pyramus, Flute as Thisby, Snout as
the Wall, Starveling as Moonshine, and Snug
as the Lion.

QUINCE: Ladies and gentlemen, perhaps you wonder at this show but, wonder on, till truth make all things plain. This man is Pyramus, if you would know. This beauteous lady is Thisby. This man doth present a wall, that vile wall, and through the wall's chink, poor souls, they are content to whisper. This man with lantern presenteth Moonshine. For by moonshine did these lovers think to meet at Ninus' tomb, there, there to woo. This grisly beast, Lion by name, the trusty Thisby, coming first by night, did scare away, and as she fled, her mantle she did let fall. Which lion vile with bloody mouth did stain. Anon comes Pyramus, sweet youth and tall, and finds his trusty Thisby's mantle stained, whereupon with his sword he bravely stabbed himself. And Thisby, tarrying in mulberry shade, his dagger drew and died. For all the rest, let Lion, Moonshine, Wall, and lovers twain, at large discourse while here they do remain.

Exit Prologue, Pyramus, Thisby, Lion,
and Moonshine.

THESEUS: I wonder if the lion will speak?

WALL: In this same interlude it doth befall, that I, one

Snout by name, present a wall. And such a wall that had in it a crannied hole or chink, through which the lovers, Pyramus and Thisby, did whisper often very secretly.

Re-enter Pyramus.

THESEUS: Pyramus draws near the wall.

PYRAMUS: I fear my Thisby's promise is forgot. And thou O wall, O sweet, O lovely wall that standest between her father's ground and mine, show me thy chink to blink through with my eye. (*Wall holds up his fingers.*) Thanks, courteous wall. But what see I? No Thisby do I see. O wicked wall, curst be thy stones for thus deceiving me.

THESEUS: The wall, methinks, being sensible should curse back at him.

BOTTOM: No, in truth, sir, he should not. "Deceiving me" is Thisby's cue. She is to enter now, and I am to spy her through the wall. You shall see it will fall pat as I told you. (*Enter Thisby.*) Yonder she comes.

THISBY: O wall, full often hast thou heard my moans for parting my fair Pyramus and me. My cherry lips have often kissed thy stones.

PYRAMUS: I see a voice . . . now will I to the chink to spy and I can hear my Thisby's face. Thisby?

THISBY: My love thou art, my love I think.

PYRAMUS: Think what thou wilt, I am thy lover. O kiss me, through the hole of this vile wall.

THISBY: I kiss the wall's hole, not your lips at all.

PYRAMUS: Wilt thou at Ninny's tomb meet me straight-away?

THISBY: I come without delay.

Exit Pyramus and Thisby.

WALL: Thus have I, Wall, my part discharged so, and, being done, thus Wall away doth go. (*Exits.*)

HIPPOLYTA: This is the silliest stuff that ever I heard.

THESEUS: Shush! (*Enter Lion and Moonshine.*) Here come two noble beasts ... a moon and a lion.

LION: Young ladies, you who fear the smallest monstrous mouse that creeps on the floor, do not quake and tremble when Lion doth roar. Then know that I, Snug the joiner, am not really a lion at all.

THESEUS: A very gentle beast and of good conscience ... Let us listen to the moon.

MOONSHINE: This lantern doth the moon represent ... myself the man in the moon do seem to be.

THESEUS: This is the greatest error of all the rest. The man should be put into the lantern. How is it else the man in the moon?

MOONSHINE: All that I have to say is to tell you that the lantern is the moon, I the man in the moon.

Re-enter Thisby.

DEMETRIUS: Silence, here comes Thisby.

THISBY: This is old Ninny's tomb. Where is my love?

LION: ROOOOOARRRR!

Thisby runs off.

DEMETRIUS: Well roared, Lion.

THESEUS: Well run, Thisby.

HIPPOLYTA: Well shone, Moon.

Lion tears Thisby's mantle and exits.

Pyramus re-enters.

PYRAMUS: Sweet moon, I thank thee for shining now so bright, for by thy gracious golden glittering beams, I trust to take of truest Thisby sight. But stay ... O spite! What dreadful dole is here? How can it be?

Thy mantle stained with blood! Approach ye furies ... O fates come, come! Crush, conclude!

THESEUS: This passion and the death of a good friend would go near to make a man look sad.

PYRAMUS: Come tears, confound. Out sword and wound the breast of Pyramus ... that left breast where heart doth hop. (*Stabs himself.*) Thus die I, thus, thus, thus. Now am I dead ... moon take thy flight. (*Exit Moonshine.*) Now die, die, die, die, die, die. (*He dies.*)

THESEUS: With the help of a surgeon he might yet recover.

HIPPOLYTA: How chance Moonshine is gone before Thisby comes back and finds her lover?

Re-enter Thisby.

THESEUS: She will find him by starlight. Here she comes to end the play.

HIPPOLYTA: I hope she will be brief.

LYSANDER: She hath spied him already with those sweet eyes.

THISBY: Asleep, my love? What, dead, my dove? O Pyramus arise! Speak ... speak! Quite dumb! Dead, dead? A tomb must cover thy sweet eyes. His eyes were green as leeks. O come trusty sword! (*Stabs herself.*) And farewell friends, thus Thisby ends. Adieu, adieu, adieu! (*Dies.*)

THESEUS: Moonshine and Lion are left to bury the dead.

DEMETRIUS: Ay, and the wall, too.

BOTTOM (*standing up*): Will it please you to see the epilogue?

THESEUS: No epilogue, I pray you, for your play needs no excuse. Never excuse, for when the players are all dead there need none to be blamed. The iron tongue of midnight hath tolled twelve. Sweet friends, to bed.

All mortals exit. Enter King Oberon,
Queen Titania, and all the fairies.

OBERON: Through the house give glimmering light, every elf and fairy sprite sing this ditty after me, and dance it trippingly.

TITANIA: Hand in hand with fairy grace, will we sing, and bless this place.

Song and dance of fairies.

OBERON: Trip away, make no stay,
Meet me all by break of day.

All exit. Enter Puck.

PUCK: If we shadows have offended, think that you but slumbered here while these visions did appear. And as I am an honest Puck, good night unto you all.